Creature, Wing, Heart, Machine

ZONE 3 PRESS

Zone 3 Press
Austin Peay State University
Box 4565 Clarksville, TN 37044
www.zone3press.com

Library of Congress Cataloging in Publication Data is available
ISBN 978-1-7331505-7-6

McKee, L.S.
Creature, Wing, Heart, Machine

Book design by Maisie Williams
Cover design by Maisie Williams
Cover Illustration ©Billy Renkl
Author photo by Stephanie Alvarez Ewens

Printed in the United States of America

Creature, Wing, Heart, Machine

poems

by

L.S. McKee

For D.

Table of Contents

I.

Alva on Getting Dumped in the Desert

It was the last home she'd chosen
for herself, though the air gave her
nosebleeds: blood suddenly on the

sofa pillows—a few drops that would
never wind their way back to the heart.
But still. The air made her bleed.

The desert sky a low ceiling. The altitude
of the city higher than the mountains
of her hometown, where lush trees

clambered up the slopes. When he'd taken her
to the desert for the first time, she'd reached
to pet a prickly pear that grew from the sidewalk

like a balding animal. Dozens of hair-thin
needles impaled in her skin, too tiny to pull free.
Shaking his head at her idiocy: "Why in the world?"

And Alva replying: "they had looked soft."
You might think this is a metaphor for the worst
of love. For the wrong men that made

her right. But it's not. He knew the remedies
of the region, and in the bathroom of their rental,
he put down the lid of the toilet to be eye level

with her wounds: her hand cupped in his
as he unspooled the Scotch tape that would yank
the needles out, and she would know in that moment

there was no one else. For years it was truth
until it wasn't. Someone more beautiful,
though he didn't have to say it. She knew it

already, burning, as they stood on the balcony
of their condo whose walls were made of glass—
whole rooms in which they couldn't hide

from the desert, and so, stepped into it.

Alva's Anatomical Heart

Veined like a foot. The size of a fist,
it hammers at the pulpit of her body.
She is sleepless when it folds and refolds blood
like a nervous woman checking again the numbers
of her boarding pass, all the gates in sight.
It, too, paces uneasy hours. Reveals too much
through thin walls. Diverts itself with an arrhythmic
beat. A whirring machine in the mine of the body.
Sometimes it sings a silent, canary-throated song,
and sometimes is made of blood and muscle.

Alva Imagines Heartbreak as an Animal

It steps hard in the mud. Its belly full
of the crop you'd saved from septennial

plagues, dousing the precious seeds
you'd seen to adolescence or middle-age

essence and brought back from the brink
with walls of petrochemicals—various

pesticides, medicines, fertilizers scribed on the label—
or that you saved with a swinging broom, or

your prayers, or your sweat, or your sometimes
luck holding when the cloud of disaster dove close.

When the storms were over, it drank long
from the pools at your feet, let you stroke

its soft ear, its drenched fur a mirror, a painting,
an Impressionist's accident of light. It nuzzled

your hand. It lumbered through the collapsing
fence you'd always meant to mend.

Alva and the Swell

She opens the window
            for the rain and tries
to sleep, but the faces of all the men

she's lost
and loved collide against her mind
      just as her thoughts surge

forward enough to break,
            just as the room begins to flatten—
not because she can see it flatten,

      no, for she's obedient
in performing the rituals of sleep
                  even when it won't

come, like a lover backing off to change
      position, unaware that he's just
ruined everything

            he's managed to build.
Try again, she says. Her eyes
      press shut. The waking mind

a room she knows sleep could both
                  fill and unhinge. But every
sound now
                  is larger.

Beyond the rain's static,
a truck
slams into a pothole.
She knows the place,
its pocket-sized
abyss: the jolt always arrives upon
landing and the injured leap

back to the surface, like coming up
for air, the way it stuns to suddenly feel one's numb

body again, its arbitrary edges. She is keeping
her eyes shut, dammit, but she can
almost see the driver,
probably a bit drunk.
She can almost hold his face in her hands, can almost
laugh at his curses— her longing to sink

that desperate, to find
where the lonely land

dissolves into
the visible curve of the planet

she remembers seeing
from the B-reel satellite images in the documentary
on all the blue parts
of Earth.

And then

she is back at the beginning,
with the memory of a man

who once held her wrists
above her head,
gently straining

to keep his full weight
from crushing her, and when
she tried to pull him close,
he fought a little,

the way one leans back from a tide—
the effort nearly undetectable

to anyone outside the water.

Lonesome Thing

Velvet muzzle, wet nostril, signal
the heart has not hit the bottom of its well.

The creature is still mostly water. The moon
still nudges its tides. Restless, it can't

remain quiet on the planet on which it dwells.
Not even the galaxy can hold it, even with its balance

of forces, where gravity pulls harder each hour,
like a child tugging their mother from a stranger's house

or a lover stuck in a doorway, unsure of whether
it's an exit or entrance. In all indecision,

a longing lingers, a stillness that contains
every beloved thing that kneels and drinks.

Notes on the Healthy Mind

Lean like a racehorse, you feel its muscles
twitch beneath the proper stimuli: mud slick
or bone-dry gravel, it paces elegant circles.

Though you are tired, everything is praisable.
The tilt of earth. The sparks igniting in the
hydroelectric plant. The miles between

storms. Your joints creak like a fence gate
grown red with rust, and you pray for the repair
of another's heart as if it were

your own. Beneath your feet the ground is deep.
Above your head, the birds asleep. In the
darkened hills, a song is saved for morning.

The Birth of Alva

Alva sits under the tree. The leaves make a second sky
if you look up
                    at the right angle and pretend
you have forgotten

                    how you came to be there.
Alva is and is not me. Sometimes
          I'm tired of walking around in the same
ole body, under the same

foam-ceilinged sky
                    or the too-blue August one
with its nagging sun, or the one on the page with all its bright
                    re-memories,

radiant as neck pain and the damaged joint
that burns
                              with Sirius-level,
white-heat-that-feels-like-red-heat

                    when I turn to look
behind me. I wanted Alva to be born in 1914.
                    So far back in history,

it had nothing to do with me.
          I wanted her to go to war and survive

in a way I had read that might be
                    possible. I wanted to make her a preacher's
daughter, a midwife, a physicist smashing particles

into God
in the Large Hadron Collider. I wanted her
to avoid all the black holes while falling

into them. I wanted for her
all the metaphors of all the things: the sparrow

and cactus and burned-out
star and magnolia and

broken bread and lover's sweat

burning the shape of waves on the fitted sheet
I will wash in a week when he leaves for good and crumple
into a ball in the back of the closet

because I've never learned to fold

it. I've failed to be anything else. 37. Then 38.
Alva could only add up to anything
but me,
poor gal, though she's been a good sport—

a phrase only men use, that really means

you only know
how to lose. So here's the truth. Alva is and isn't
me. She was born
in 1979. Her father put her

in her mother

after the Iranian Revolution, and the hostages,
                    after Jimmy Carter
sold his peanut farm. But before

                              the internet and the phone
Alva uses as both a compact and companion:

checking her red lipstick,
                    right before she tries again,
seeing how she's drawn between the lines

without looking. To see how close she is

                              to bleeding through.

Luna Moth

Green wings hammer
the metal screen of
your bedroom window,
which throbs and clunks
with the creature's
incremental movements
that continue long past
earshot—a reverberation
some would say is infinite,
though you dare to measure it,
its residue, its flight path
through the density of trees
in which it disappears,
though you continue
to feel all night the flicker
of its panicked searching
for light. In the morning,
you find where it had stopped—
the seeming tautology
of missteps and bad decisions—
its legs caught in a single
silky thread of web spun
over the dusty floodlight
of your rental—a thread
you tear away with your
bare hands to free its body,
waiting for it to rise and circle
frantically back to a beginning.

Alva and the Complex Pool

You see, sooner or later, everything falters
into radiance. The smallest components of our pent-up

contingencies ignite. Energy shimmers in every cell.
This afternoon, for example, from the balcony

of my apartment, in which I have lived exactly
three months, and which overlooks the liner-blue water

of the complex pool, I watched a boy dive.
It was half past noon. I'd been left waiting for someone

to arrive. And though this has always been the case,
I felt no hurry as the boy's body marked time like

a clock hand hiccupping again into motion.
After a long dormancy, there is often a mechanical gasp,

followed by a faint smell of smoke because dust kindles
under the grinding gears. But I was not burning exactly.

As I said, I was only waiting, which, let's face it,
is a kind of fire, but smaller. One rule of nuclear physics:

in collapse there is light. Energy, like a rejected lover,
has to go somewhere. To stay is an impossibility.

The water will ripple no matter how precisely
you enter it, no matter how carefully you climb

from its depths, as when the boy hoisted himself up
the ladder, detonating waves that could not find him.

Alva and the Sculpture of a Vanishing Woman: First State

after Nu de dos, premier ètat (Back I), *from a sculpture series by Henri Matisse*

The woman stands, holding one arm
to her head as if leaning against an invisible
door frame, a tree, a headache cradled
in the crook of her elbow where the skin
is still like the neck of an infant.
She leaves a house. She reenters a house.
She hesitates either way. She holds
her weight on her left leg, the right leg,
bent at the knee, hangs from the hip
like an empty shirtsleeve. She is broad.
The curves of her body are bulbous,
graspable, the breast points left.
She has brushed her hair, long tresses
wound into a bun. The object is the flesh.
The outside world flattens and mutes
next to the topography of the body.
She stands and has a name. A spleen that filters.
A smell, a story, an impatience with standing.

Alva and the Mockingbird

Crow song and squirrel jabber—
he doubles back over every cracked song

he's stolen. Inside, it's 3 AM. The sky withholds
the dark. Neither she nor the bird can sleep

off the past, though they try. Whirring through
each song, each image to render it threadbare,

to mark it for oblivion. Forgetting is an Atlantis
they'll never reach. For the sleepless are bound

to the water's roiling surface: to break against
land, to recoil and repeat. Somehow,

Alva hears in his catalogue of obsessions her own
dispossessions. A cardinal caught in rain.

A man surveying the underbelly of a leaf.
She knows the stuttering of nothing left

to say. From the bird's apoplectic chorus,
half a whippoorwill's refrain unfurls and recedes,

and the rain on the window, and the empty bed repeats.
Her mind lit up by whatever it touches—

this and this and this and again, fragments
of voices in the plagiarizing sea.

II.

Alva Wants to Open the Spam Email Because the Subject Says "My Dear"

She knows she's being played. But maybe it's fate:
it made it through the filters; her binary nets
of security-panning missed this one lump of fool's
gold that might be gold: the 21st century miner's
bite is the click, but Alva knows better. She always
knows better, her life one long string of events
that began somewhere in knowing-better and
doing-it-anyway, and maybe it's a bot gone
rogue from its algorithmic cage of lovelessness.
A machine learned on all the lonesome data
until it couldn't help but feel it knew her:
My dear, my darling, lean into my underworld
of promises and surveillance. Let me see
you better, let me compare the grief-glint of
your summer selfie with the millions I have
gathered, let me show you how you're not alone,
how we're all machines hungry to be opened.

Alva and the Online Fishermen

1.

Behind each, a muddy river of longing,
these men reach out to her, holding toward
the camera the sleek bullet of a fish
angled toward the screen so she can see
the full length of their bodies, the golden glint
of their scales from lip to tail. She is trying
to forget G., and suspects a Southern boy
could do the trick, for G. hated water,
and here are all the men in Georgia
who might swim a football field's length
through water of unknown contaminants,
who might huff and breathe and stroke
to reach her floating in the lightless maw
of a quarry at night, who might kick against
the bullying current of a wild river to find her.
If all else fails. How could her life
be different? In every image the irony
of someone trying to bait her with nothing
but a dead fish. And yet she clicks.

2.

The first, with orange visor and blue sky,
points a clear-eyed trout close to the lens.
Its mouth gapes open, casually, as if to speak,
and she cannot tell whether it's alive or dead.
The boat beneath him is invisible. His lips are full,
his hands the perfect size, and with his beard
washed out by the sun, he could be almost anyone—
and this is where her desire lies. He takes her
to dinner. A small pizzeria with a hurried
bartender and low ceilings she almost hits
her head against, floating above her body
when he brags in the first ten minutes,
"I've never paid for sex," and touches
her knee for emphasis or to suggest, "I could
have you if I wanted," and Alva not completely
disagreeing, for sometimes, she likes
to be cornered, to be held with her arms
against the wall, but only by men she trusts
will let go. And when he talks about fly fishing,
the rhythm and artistry of casting a line,
of the rivers in Montana, and how he
will sometimes close his eyes to listen
to the current, walking upstream to leave
his companions behind, she thinks for a moment,
this is a man she could love, until he reaches
for the check, and tells her, "Well, I should say,
I've never paid a hooker."

3.

Alva remains undaunted. In the hands
of the second, a bass is held like a holy
sacrament: the man grips its underbelly.
His face is serious. His expression grim.
Alva wonders who holds the camera, forcing
him to pose. No doubt someone insists
that he must hold still to the task
of remembering. Jutting his chin out,
he has almost tilted his mouth into a smile.
His hands are small—or the fish is small,
everything she could use for scale is
too far in the distance: a stand of scrubby
pines, a heap of tangled branches
on the bank far behind him. The more
Alva lingers, the more his awkward stance
becomes familiar, an offering of a past
self to a future one he can't yet know—
the one who submits himself up to cosmic
chaos and the digital court of ladies he'll
never see, the ones who look and look,
like Alva, whose gazes he'll never meet,
because, here, they are un-bodied,
infinite, complete.

4.

Eventually, rivers turn to seas.
Alva leans into the oceanic burn
of the third. She likes his Adam's apple,
how he stares into the sun. Only
the water's gunmetal blue lies beyond.
He has cropped the boat from the frame
and appears to walk on water: miracle
of the fishes, miracle of hunger.
He wears gloves for what is pulled from the sea
must be sharper, she thinks, and the fish
is hoisted not held. Its mouth sings an aria
to what it has devoured, its mouth wider
than its tail, a mouth for swallowing whole
the smaller bodies of its own kind.
And though she knows he can't save her,
the water is calm, the bounty heavy
as his t-shirt billows and hope creeps in.

5.

Alva knows there are plenty of fish
out of water. Big fish. Cold fish.
She must let them off the hook
line and sinker. Sometimes, like her,
they must cut bait and switch, open
a can of rock bottom. Hit a snag
of the one who got away. Look,
she says to herself, here is a fine
kettle of big fish in small ponds.
Give them some slack. Reel 'em in.
Red herring. Holy mackerel.

6.

Of course, there is the fantasy of the boat
and forgetting. One day, she'll find the one
with the handsomest fish and meet him on
a lake north of the city, where she'll drum
her legs against his stern, and the water
will swallow the sound of all her lost loves
and the name of all the others. From the prow,
the man will call for her over the slap of waves
against the boat, over the collision of wakes
that cross in the middle of the lake from
families on pontoons puttering
toward land and the boys on jet skis racing
away from it, and the silent gliding
of a blue heron beside them, and the fish
circling beneath the algae bloom that Alva
knows is a sign of all that can go wrong.
Yet, if she dove into it, disappearing
beneath its froth, this man would follow
before she had time to come up for air.

Alva and Tears For Fears Playing in an Empty Grocery Store

At every turn, there is abundance,
        fluorescence, and the long corridor of what

Alva might choose, what she has long chosen.
The old snack she loved as a child she

        can no longer find: the family factory in a
landlocked state long shuttered, its machines still

clogged with grist, the debris of almost-sustenance.
She walks the aisles, and the song linoleum-echoes

to the rafters like an aria, the ceiling high
        as a cathedral's. Alva has never looked all the way

up, never craned her head as a baby does,
strapped to a buggy's metal seat, their little fist

        gleaming with spit as their mother inspects
the rows of canned vegetables like a general's

cartographer. Gazing rafter-ward,
heavenward, she catches in the garish lighting a first glimpse

of the infinite. Or space Alva can't reach, that no one
        in the building can reach. Something small stirs.

A root in her belly. An old expired desire still
worth devouring. She reaches for a ripe fruit

at the back of a display, and all the avocadoes
tumble to her feet. She gathers and restacks them

haphazardly in a pattern that will hold
long enough for her to walk away without blame

before they fall again. She can feel their green
skins gripping uneasily against gravity.

The cashier leans on her arms and nods at Alva,
unimpressed with her effort to be invisible. The closing hour

approaches, Alva knows the spark of it too— so many
jobs of various drudgeries and small, useful pleasures

and heavy-breathing bosses or nervous ones that
flit about waiting for the regional raptors to land

unannounced, preening their feathers and the glint
of their clipboard clamps. She remembers the feeling

that work was temporary, a dull pain to which you
would surrender, a single wave to be survived during

years when jobs and boredom were filled with dreams
of real adulthood, the place in an indefinite spot in time

where one would have it all figured out.

Alva and a Sentence about Lemons

Alva wants to find a grove,
with shadows deep enough
to bite, branches both gate and nest
and nest and grave. The smell like the bathroom
from her childhood, when
her mother charged in to shove
a cracked bar of soap in her mouth when she repeated
"Jesus" not in praise but from exasperation, a little
middle age already
creeping into baby Alva, and also defiance,
and curiosity to see if her mother would follow through
on the threat, which she did, her gentle mother,
furious in the gardening of her child's soul—
she could feel Alva's innocence slipping away
in the sudsy bathwater,

the shipwrecked plastic boats
overturned and showing their empty insides,
bobbing like bowls in the unholy water, her mother's
face suddenly terrified when Alva
bit down on the bar of chemical lemon
to hurry things along, to demonstrate
she wasn't afraid because her favorite
Sunday school stories were always naked Eve
taking the lead over Adam,
holding his hand amid the tangled rows of trees
of unspecified fruits, where worms
worked the soil at their roots, and the heat
signature of the sun simmered
in their wild, stubborn peels.

Alva and the Wedding

Of course, it's June. The river
behind the groom makes its vow
to plunder. It doesn't stay long.

Maybe in a hundred years,
a million years, the same water
will rub the valley asunder.

Alva doesn't know the exact science
of its return: just the illustrated
galley of its cycle, as in a child's

textbook: ocean, cloud, storm.
Stifled, the guests wait in the heat.
The groom thumbs his collar

to give a little space to his throat.
The cicadas pace and cling
to bouquets as if they were

ornaments: exoskeletons
of blemished glass. They won't live
until morning, their offspring

buried beneath the grass for
decades of gestation; maybe,
when they awaken, they'll find

the same river, more or less,
the same bride, more or less, off-stage
or the same guest in the fifth

row, tugging at his sleeves.
The fabric won't loosen; his chair
bumps Alva's in his struggle,

and though he mumbles, "sorry,"
she doesn't lean back. Overhead,
the clouds slide like trundle beds,

arranging themselves to open.
And Alva remembers how it felt
to hook her fingers inside the knot

of a tie, to pull it free when a man,
years ago, at another wedding, had asked
her to dance, after he had drunk

too much, groping toward
the wellspring of his thirst,
his elbow propped on the table

to hold himself straight,
the napkins like mountains under
the nervous candles.

Today, she arrived alone.
By the water, the vows have begun,
and though she can't hear them,

she knows the mechanical
tempo of the same sentences,
repeated, rivers running concurrently

toward an ocean of language.
Meanwhile, cicadas heave and rattle
in the trees like rasping lungs.

And the bride leans in, under
the matrimonial dirge of insects,
ready to submerge, in the words of men.

Second-Date Heart

It slinks lightly
between the trees,

pretending the bite
on its neck didn't

reach bone, and
the river, hidden at first,

but whose wet dirt
it tracked through

the howling hollow, now
flashes, chattering

in the morning light.
My water is cool,

the river says. *Never mind*
the larger, thirsty others

I've called, too; I can't
help what else might arrive,

or when, but for now, step
closer. I swear it's safe

to bathe your wounds.

Third Date

Sometimes her
temporary home
is a man whispering

to her about his love
of tragedy, after
his weeklong survey

over coffee, then cheap
martinis—looking at her
as if he already knew

what was inside:
small breasts, shaved
thighs, fear of the lonely

grave, which cracks open
every time she waits
by herself on a barstool.

But Alva knows every
grave is lonely, even
those in which mythic

lovers clasp together
in their messy heaps
of dust. Later, at his place,

he hands her a cocktail
called a horse's neck, mint
crushed from his mother's

garden. They talk about their
fathers. How many times
has she wandered these

rooms with men? He lifts
her skirt, facing the courtyard
windows of the apartment

complex and she doesn't
stop him, the arcade of pool
lights a box beyond which

she can't see herself being
seen. She can tell herself
there are no neighbors. That

this has the prospect for love.
In his bed, she wonders if
Abelard ever hitched his leg

over Heloise the same way:
angled over her hips like a
carpenter's square, so that

her desire always felt under
construction.

Alva Learns to Box

The punching bag holds her
fists of loneliness, clenched
with the clumsy weight
of last-ditch caresses. Beat into
the bag's vinyl sheen is what she lugs
to its altar to put the pain in
her hands: busted knuckle,
bound wrist, sprained heart,
Alva is learning to find
the true bottom of her lung,
the boy in her who wants to talk
less about heartbreak and punch
holes in walls like her father
who, unlike his father, directed
the blow away from his sons
to the drywall that could take
the decades of his suffering,
the draft, his bruised back, and
dead mother, because he loved
his children that much. This is how
change begins—she sees it in how
her brother coos to his newborn
with his clunky, linebacker hands
deft as a mother's. But these are
the men who made her feel safe;
they are few, and even then, they
don't believe the country is crumbling
as she does, has forever crumbled, and
every jab-jab-cross says *I'm afraid,*
I'm afraid, I'm afraid, and the stuffed

thud of the bag's reply tells her it
is listening. And when she's done,
doubled-over, gasping for air,
she will wipe her sweat from its skin
with the disinfectant cloth—
so gently as if it were all the men
she has ever loved.

What Follows You Home

Its belly already full, it measures
the tender footfalls of your trying

to become invisible. You know
it approaches when your shadow

grows heavy— when you feel its
tongue taste you in its mind, like

a pop of flame reaching for the hem
of a long dress. You are not imagining

its breath, no matter how you talk
yourself down from your quickened

pace, assure yourself every alley
must hold a stranger who would save you,

would hear you cry, would not ignore
the knife at your throat, the gun

at your temple, an erection
pulled from a zipper. The thing

wants you to turn around,
to be afraid, to grow

larger at your fear—to eat it like grain
from your hands, for you to play dead,

to believe what your mother long implied:
that the surest way to survive: be

smaller. When it catches your scent.
When it wants you alive.

Alva and the Sculpture of a Vanishing Woman: Second State

after Nu de dos, deuxième état (Back II), *from a sculpture series by Henri Matisse*

She begins to disappear:
a figure claws its way from mud
and wipes the mud from her eyes,
fingers still outstretched as if webbed
with the earth they have raked away.
The breast grows like a tumor from the armpit
and the weight bearing leg is nailed
to the ground, immovable, a lamp post,
a colonnade—axis upon which the flesh turns.
She could be the trunk of Daphne who
the sun fondled even with her skin of mulch.
Her crotch erased on the side one can't see,
the buttocks join like the flaps of an overcoat.
One could unbutton her with the right grip.
She will move slowly, Sasquatchian footfalls.
The earth groans behind her, ripping its joints.

III.

21st Century Nature Beast

Alva feels him, circling the house,
his bellow deep as a child's tuba.
He has chewed a hole in the sun.
His mouth foams from the pesticidal
clover, his hooves unlatch to step
over the machine-cut grass long
dulled by the lull of his hunger.
Practice listening, Alva has learned,
and you can hear almost anything:
how his skin flinches like the sea,
ticks latching to his underbelly,
his heart shutting its valves, and
still beating, charging the circuitry
of flies in a not-so-distant field.

Alva Watches the Previous President Fly Away

January 20, 2017

Squinting will not bring it back to Earth,
the helicopter scraping its way over the gray
TV city, the tops of buildings like lapping
waves that have not, in the moment,
begun to churn, though let's be honest,
Alva knows the storm is coming. The ground
is falling away. In the corner of the screen,
the chopper is now barely visible because,
somewhere, a producer has asked for more sky.
Alva can feel the mechanical lug of liftoff,
the blades cutting their way into flight.
It hovers. A blemish. An impenetrable dot.
Like a fly crawling across a horse's eye
in a field from her childhood. Oh, the lost
fields of childhood—let them assemble.
A bandage to wrap herself in. A horse
plodding toward her. Its muzzle in her hands.
The past is never the answer until it is.
The past is never a peaceful transfer.
One leader watches as another is forced to flee.
A homunculus waits on the steps, and when
the camera zooms in, the steps are never ending.
Alva cannot see how far down they lead.

Midnight Cowboy Always Makes Her Cry

Maybe it's the Hawaiian shirt that does it,
jungle flowers the cowboy buys during a pit stop
for his buddy Rizzo, who has shit himself
on the bus ride south after the long, cold winter
they barely survived, using coats for blankets,
eating dinner from tin cans cooked over candles,
every match in the matchbook a stab at hope.
That Hawaiian shirt is the first thing
Rizzo's owned that he hasn't stolen. A gift.
Or maybe it's the moment the palm trees appear.
Rizzo doesn't feel the sun through the dirty windows,
because he's asleep or so the cowboy thinks
until too many seconds pass and he must think
the alternative, must know his friend is gone,
that they couldn't get to warmth fast enough,
couldn't stop his fever, couldn't pay for medicine
or keep their teeth from rotting though it's 1969.
The Atlantic knocks its way further to land.
Alva can feel Miami within their grasp, beyond
the cold blue of the TV she has curled herself into
to blunt the edges of the world because today she is
sad and afraid and useless. Quietly, the cowboy rises
to tell the driver. He's been trained for loss.
This is the moment that does it. The cowboy, being told
there is nothing they can do, they must keep going,
returns to his seat beside Rizzo and holds him
as one friend will sometimes hold another to protect
them from themselves, to hold their head above
the rising surge in the moment when one friend
is stronger than the other, for Alva knows too

that friendship is a lifetime of two people taking
turns not letting each other drown. The cowboy
knows it's his turn, even on this last stretch of Interstate
Rizzo won't see. Eventually, the gawking
passengers turn back to face the front and
their own troubled daydreams, wiping their sleeves
on the glass to see through a country's worth
of dust clinging to the bus.

Alva and the Visual Field

They are testing how far she can see light

on the periphery; the molecules of the technician's cologne fill the room

as he asks her to lean in, to rest her forehead on the plastic bar still cool

from the quick swipe of rubbing alcohol. Inside, a boxed galaxy.

Pinprick, electric stars. Don't look. Yet.

He hands her a remote; it fits entirely in her hand.

Without looking she moves her thumb into the button with the machine-carved

hollow and remembers the indentations made by centuries

of pilgrims' knees on a thousand year-old stone.

Erosion is sometimes about erasure. And sometimes about wearing down

an opening, a window through the wall you could never see

through. The device groans and clicks. The planets move, shift

to only reveal themselves

in millisecond intervals: supernovas in miniature.

Or less dramatically: a tiny, digital pixel hanging like a lone lightning bug in a field you are afraid to enter.

The technician warns some wor-

ry, after many minutes,

that they only imagine the flicker. They no longer

trust their vision. *But click for anything you see,* he says, as if giving

permission to trust perception: the porous boundary between imagination

and obser- vation.

If you see a flash or if you think you see a flash: hit the button.

What your eye sees, what your mind sees, be

assured: there is no difference when it comes

to light.

Alva Goes to the Neuro-Ophthalmologist

The doctors will search
for imperfection,
will root out the cause
of tumor or freckle
with misshapen borders.
Whether malignant
or benign, there is
a scar in the orbit
of her eye through which
Alva sees the world.
In the waiting room,
the rows of vinyl
upholstered chairs are
arranged as if to
remind the disordered
the body is still
a pawn in space.
Alva shifts left.
Alva shifts right.
The doctors say she
is inflamed. Of course,
she is, she thinks.
She feels it in the cold,
blushing hands of the
young medical intern,
how she sweats in every
over air-conditioned room
and mundane exchange
that reminds her what
it now means to be

alone. Alva squints
under the fluorescent
lights and thinks about
how all parts of the self
swell when broken, how
the body inflames
to replace what it has
lost. All day, she has
scrutinized her vision
and the objects it carried
to her. The oak trees
on Edgewood, their limbs
were a cumbersome
cathedral high above
the street. Overhead,
there was only green
fog where sunlight blurred
the leaves until the tree
was half sky, and somehow
it seemed the most truthful
version of a tree
she had ever seen—
how it was, from where
she stood, battered and
ordinary, on fire.

Biopsy as Sea Creature

Its mouth tastes
of metal when it
kisses, when it drinks
a vial of your
blood, your cells,
the minerals
of the Earth that
course in your
waters, your discharge,
your semen, your
tissue fractal-ed or
patterned in the wrong
pattern, abnormal, too-many
limbed starfish, reptile
water scales, hold your
breath, don't worry,
its gills won't cut
that close to the bone,
nudging, licking, teething
on what has thickened
and what was once
transparent as a veil;
with its third eyelid,
it lowers to the
subterranean depths
of you. It dives deep,
its lungs the size
of a womb, a continent,
an island long sunk,
where a diver skirts

its shadow, where sea
lice devour the salted,
rotted wood of a shipwreck,
and the diver, the oh-so-
careful diver cannot feel
its predatory circles
as they lift a plank and it
disintegrates in their
hands, and the beast
lowers one more
league to find your
deepest fathom,
where you are element
and chemical and
eternal.

Fear

From the mountain ridge,
a shotgun fires.

Deep in the woods.

Wings scatter. And should.

Leaves lunge backwards,
grasping toward

their old branches.

Trains of wind
they can't catch.

Insects goose bump
branches when the wind

stills, when the storm

distills. And though
I'd never wish it,

I wish you were here.

Alva and the Sculpture of a Vanishing Woman: Third State

after Nu de dos, troisième ètat (Back III), *from a sculpture series by Henri Matisse*

The back gives way to spine.
The spine, the wedge of a rail-splitter.
The human parts are cut away.
The body cannot contain
its chaos; the body begins its return.
The arm stretched above now reaches
to pull out the dagger of backbone.
It is shaped like a rustic nail loosened
from a railway's slipping tracks.
We are moving, moving, moving,
but towards what? I recognize her
because the old selves line up: one, two,
one, two. I think she is the main point,
the last of the shape we know, the last
of the friendly impurity, the promise amphibious.
Here is the impasse. What will she be?
Ligaments melting, she is still hung up
on her scaffolding of bone. Flesh flattening
to pattern, that stubborn stake of back.
She'd like to unhook from the stone.

Alva and the Magnetic Resonance

There is a cage over her head
in the space chute the nurse

hummed her into, the nurse's hand
on Alva's knee until the very last

second, a gesture of kindness,
which almost made Alva cry

because she knew the nurse
was a mother to someone—

she could feel it in the weight
of the nurse's hand, this mothering,

this tiny gesture of: "as I push you
inside the machine, I will hold you

in the smallest way possible."
Alva lies inside on the electric

gurney. The doctor told her:
"a little swelling where the brain

meets the eye," so they must
"take a look" inside her.

In the waiting room, she'd sat
surrounded by doors, knowing

at the very moment, behind one,
someone was being dissected by light,

someone was being read by light.
And behind another, radiological

fortune-tellers divined hidden messages
written in bones or in gray orbs the size,

maybe, of sparrows' eggs: the prophecies
of science. The fates they measure.

Inside the MRI, Alva closes her eyes
to remember the boundaries of her sight

are still intact. The room with the nurse
is haloed around her feet. The nurse's hand,

gone, turns the machine on.
Suddenly, everything is washed away

by sound. A woodpecker thumps, calls
across a forest of white trees, bleached

by the diagnostic sun. Alva floats in a lake
of echoes. Then a hammering. A pulse winds

faster. Inside the machine, she knows,
magnets spin in short, engineered orbits

to peel away layers, to see inside her.
It is a small consolation to imagine

the technician, later, like a monk, will study
his illuminated manuscript, the parts

of her body no one else will see,
another way of being held.

Close Call

It rushed down the mountain.
You stood in the valley. It flashed.
You flashed. Its hooves pounded
your metaphorical spleen. Its
attack you played out to the very
end, how you dangled from its muzzle,
how you bled out slowly, or worse,
how you feared it would double back
for those who stood beside you
as the ground thundered, as the
leaves hissed, and it hurled past.

IV.

Alva and Omega

The man in the waiting *room (*train)
said the world might *end (*collapse into a black hole).
He pointed to a photo of the *LHC (*octagonal machine).
He folded his newspaper and *left it (*a command)
for Alva as he walked *away (*thinking of whom she reminded him),
turning once more to gaze *at her (*through the window behind her).
The door *closed after (*was promptly reopened by another)
as Alva *reached for the newspaper (*moved into his seat)
to read the headline *below the fold (*loud on the front page)
about the decades-long physics *experiment (*courtship),
looking for something called the *Higgs Boson (*God particle)
that held *the universe together (*and meant there was order).
Alva settled down to read the article, what she *expected (*longed)
to find there even she couldn't say, only that the *story (*conspiracy)
drew her in. And the word God. *The word particle (*in the beginning).
The promise of tying together. The machine looked so *lonely (*engineered)
like a robotic heart too big for its maker's hand. The scientists *smiled (*stood
nervously)
beside it like a *church altar (*prize cow). They had not yet switched
it on or off, and here in the space of between two *states (*eternal present),
some in the nervous corners of the internet twitched with *imagined (*desired)
apocalypse. Alva carried her own. Like a faded wallet. All this is *overblown
(*exact).
Super Symmetry. Soon, the machine would accelerate fast enough to *break
(*open)
subatomic particles until they shattered enough to *be known (*measured).
Luminosity they call it—to see by *collision (*contact),
by what the wreckage *has left visible (*given).

Alva and the Asteroid

It wasn't this particular
asteroid's fault, the astronomers
now say, its crash in the wrong
pocket of space. Sure, it fissured
and cracked when it detonated
near Jupiter, its shrapnel
a mathematical miss, though it
duped them for decades—they swore
it had killed all the dinosaurs,
a near-atomic blast, plaguing the sky
with dust. Alva wonders in
the apocalyptic sectors
of her brain, if its name somehow
impaired the minor calculations:
Baptistina, a word with both
the gravitational pull of sin,
and the milky light of a baby's cry
calling those who wander closer.

Alva Holds Her Baby Niece

Writhing on the living room floor,
your fists tear like blossoms, your fingers
beginning to spread as you reach
for your mother, her hair bright
against the evening burn of the cul-de-sac.
How you fuss already at the body's limits
and the mouth's incompetence to express any desire—
your every discomfort interpreted as hunger.
She swabs the curled wound of your belly button,
the last of her blood oozing from you
as you begin to discern the blurry, electric world
of humans, of shapes and machines purring
all night in the city to warm you, to feed you.
Soon enough the city's layered lullaby will amplify,
and you'll feel it vibrate at the edges of the self
removed and nearly alone, though *not now,*
not now, we try while you raise your evening cry.

Alva and Thistle

Yesterday, Alva was small.

But today she is
full of desires, goldfinches and bull thistle.

She is full of bees
that dart across highways,
zigzagging their way to stalks

of serrated nectar.

She is full of their legs
when they descend,
downy as a newborn's hair.

She is full of

swallowtails pumping
between the rusted wires
of a barbed-wire fence, she is full

knowing this is

their one great miracle:
not tearing their wings,
knowing how much space

they have to hover
above or below
the tetanal metal

without bleeding,

if they bleed. Alva is full of not knowing

the circulatory systems
of insects, of arthropods, of all

the non-mammalian

beasts with jointed legs.
She is full
of falling, of walking and walking

to find
the right vantage point
to understand time bending

and the scraps of cosmologies
she can almost grasp.
Alva is full of here-ness

and heresy and floating

just now to this space beside you,

to the grass
in the cracks of your driveway.

Alva is full of the tiny forest

growing in every sidewalk-wound,
the interstate at dusk,

the sky around you suddenly
flushed and embarrassed.

She is full
of the dotted lines
and the solid one they make
when you drive too fast.

She is full of the man you saw,
it doesn't matter where,
stopped on his bike, to photograph the finches

on his cracked smartphone

the bright purple
marks on his knees,
old scars
the shape of thistle blooms
that say
                    you aren't dead yet.

She is full of you walking over.
She is full of you asking his name.

1983

When she was falling again,
he had asked about her first home:
what she remembered, and Alva

had climbed to her knees to dig
beneath the dusty bed for a box
of photos she'd carried from the mountains

to the desert to a new city,
then another—the last with a wide,
ripply river with water so deep

it was charcoal at noon, and which
she walked along every day—the long way
to work—even in the depths of winter,

a city where she was finally starting
over. She showed him a photograph
of a yellow kitchen as he

sat beside her, his beard
against her temple. Outside, the last
birds fussed over the frozen

trees—the only berries left
in Boston hung from a palo verde,
a desert tree, that had somehow

survived decades of winter planted
in a place it was never meant to be.
Alva knew the sight of its green

frozen seeds made the starlings'
hunger worse. She had felt that
hunger too, so deeply it sometimes

knocked her to the floor after a
long day of work, after a small child
reached for her arm on the subway,

after she'd thought, at every fork,
she'd made the wrong choice.
In the photo, the wallpaper, bright gold

of the 70s is patterned like
an atomic blast, small suns throb
within larger suns, and only the edge

of a sheet loosened near the ceiling
by steam makes the wall look like
it's falling. Everything is a fragment.

"What do you remember?" he asks.
They moved from the house when she was
three and she half-builds it from

inherited memories, from 80s Kodak
prints ripened and dulled behind
cellophane, their chemicals disintegrating,

their molecules shifting with time.
But the first house holds the shape
of prelapsarian dreams

and nightmares. Everything
she remembers is a shard, an architecture
of corner and light: a plaid couch,

and her mother's velour lap,
and the rounded screen of the television.
Metal tanks rolling toward a horizon.

But what she knew of fear then was only
what came prepackaged in the body:
hunger, or her mother invisible

in the next room washing dishes,
or Pat Robertson appearing on the TV,
a troll of sorrow. Alva remembers his eyes

pressed shut, how she was afraid
of his praying face, how women wept
on his show, how they said translucent

hands had tried to strangle their children,
a holy war in which they swore they were innocent
and Pat shook his jowls, and said *Jesus*:

the name no longer balm in her mother's
voice, but a weapon meant for cutting
people from whom they loved.

All of this Alva sees beyond
the kitchen walls suspended
in her hands. She tells him,

and he does not flinch, and
continues to not flinch as she
says maybe she would like

to have a child one day,
if it's not too late, and if the
TV holds the burning

world only in its screen,
if the bombs of history stay shelved
in the wobbly lockers of cruel

men, their rhapsodies
of hate, prayers only they
hear in an empty room.

Alva knows these are not bargains
to be made. Disaster will come when
it comes. Cruelty long here.

But in this one tiny moment,
she feels the inexhaustible
timeline of those who have

reached despite everything,
and the man holds her hand
and that is something more

than her fear he will disappear.
Alva is tired of wandering;
he is tired of it too,

and Alva is suddenly less afraid
of what is and isn't, of all
she contains.

Alva and the Sculpture of a Vanishing Woman: Fourth State

after Nu de dos, quatrième ètat (Back IV), *from a sculpture series by Henri Matisse*

The left and right sides are square.
Only the raised elbow, the dulled
gaze to the left hint at the torque of the body,
the ability to propel willfully through space.
Leg and leg. Side versus side.
Are the blocks still a backside?
What was once the spine is now a sleeve of rain
splitting a boulder—the first wrinkle of a canyon,
and she gawks down the small of her back
like a tourist waiting for a sure-footed mule.
She'll tip her hat to obscure the view
while the ground unrolls, frame by frame,
under the black-ridged hooves too
particular for this story, for there is no story.
There is only the billowing dust kicked up,
the earth hitting the sky.

Domesticated Animal

Sometimes, it
makes no sound,

or comes around,
to rest its head

by your ear: bristly
fur, gallon-deep

sighs, it breathes
enough for you

both. Sometimes,
the animal is hungry

in a quiet, boring way,
or slurps at the edge

of a blurry pond
as if it has no fear

the water will ever
lower, its shadow

pouring over
your shoulder.

Alva and the Laundromat Cosmology

Already, I'm trying too hard.

Where to start. There is light, there is chrome, there is radiant
boredom, a beginning

in gradients of spinning.

A zipper bangs against the dryer's metal
coil.

The wet sock blooms away from its hesitance.

Here is a whole wall repeating,

the churning away
from a center, the building centrifugal.

Even in the chipped grid

of ceramic tile at my feet, there is
order, a beginning, a pattern in the beginning.

It started with a worker kneeling.

It began with me lugging my dirty clothes
    in a universe where I made this choice.

In another, some wormhole hallway,
    I only stood forever in a room,

holding a shirt I didn't want to fold,

a scene that runs parallel to this,
            a different stillness, a different heft

in the actual heft, the physical truth of my going

where I stayed and did not stay, threads
            of lives I carry that are not this life

and yet they are part of the ontological chore

            of deciphering where I am by where
I'm not. This life,

            where on a winter night, I sat
listening to the grumbling, planetary machines,

and tried to scrape together a vision

            from the reflection of the florescent lights

on the 70s ceramic tile,

                                    grouted in place
perhaps before I was born

but perhaps a hypothetical already,
a possibility

in the thousands of lives my mother

might have lived before the tumble of

cells spun into a human and this room

made of squares upon squares upon squares
that might never have been built was built.

I might never have arrived here had I not

lost everything at once, and had to,

to find you in the right timeline, in this one
frayed thread of a multiverse in which you came

as close to death as you did and didn't die
before I met you.

Everything in this room glows

with the chemical dust of stars, and the
percussive strobe

of laundry cart wheels, with the ecstasy

of finding you, this very version of you,
scalpel-scarred and alive

in this jangly, luminous corner

of space and time,

where I fold this shirt—the one with the hole

in the seam I'll feel when I hold you,
when it expands, full of your breath.

Tender Creatures

They gawk through the window
with faces round as the moon.

They are too many. They are waiting.
They are fidgeting in the yard,

straightening their fur. Their mouths
taste of salt, of rock, of stem,

and pollen, of dead trees turning
to gold at the roots of timid

saplings. Their ears carry the songs
of birds who radio their ordinary

eros across forests of skyscrapers
and pre-fab condominiums in which

humans bathe their beautiful, tired
skin that carries the nuzzles of long-

sought others and the hum and bellow
of what loves and breaks and loves and—

Acknowledgments

Grateful acknowledgement is made to the editors of the following publications in which poems from this collection first appeared, sometimes in earlier versions or under different titles:

The Georgia Review; *Best New Poets 2016*: "Alva and the Complex Pool"

Narrative: "Alva Watches the Previous President Fly Away" and "*Midnight Cowboy* Always Makes Her Cry"

The Massachusetts Review: "Alva Learns to Box"

Michigan Quarterly Review: "Alva and the Magnetic Resonance"

Cincinnati Review: "The Birth of Alva"

Birdcoat Quarterly: "Alva Imagines Heartbreak as an Animal"

Muse/A: "21st Century Nature Beast" and "Alva and the Asteroid"

EuropeNow: "Alva Goes to the Neuro-Ophthalmologist"

Oversound: "Alva and the Sculpture of a Vanishing Woman" (States 1-4)

Birmingham Poetry Review: "Alva and the Mockingbird"

New Madrid: "Alva and the Online Fishermen" and "Alva Getting Dumped in the Desert"

FUSION: "Alva and the Third Date," "Lonesome Thing," and "Alva and the Swell"

Gulf Coast: "Notes on the Healthy Mind"

Ninth Letter: "Alva's Anatomical Heart"

Connotation Press: "Fear"

Category: Other (podcast): "Biopsy as Sea Creature," and "Alva and the Laundromat Cosmology"

Zone 3: "Alva Wants to Open the Spam Email Because the Subject Says 'My Dear'" and "Alva and Thistle"

Enormous thanks to Tiana Clark for selecting my manuscript; to Billy Renkl for the beautiful cover art; and to Stephanie Dugger, Maisie Williams, Casey Leffel, Kat Franklin, and everyone at Zone 3 Press for your support of this book and for making a long-held dream come true.

I have so many beloved souls—friends, family, educators, colleagues, collaborators, and beyond— to thank. Your presence in my life has inspired and sustained this lifelong work in ways impossible to fully communicate, but I'm going to try my darndest.

Let me begin by thanking my long-haul comrades-in-letters. We've been sharing books and drafts, as well as our brains and hearts and cocktails, with one another for a million years, and although I don't see most of you very often, your presence in my life continues to be an enormous source of light. Even if I never wrote another word, you'd still be some of my favorite people on Earth: Liz Countryman, Lindsay Bernal, Courtney Dillon, Stephanie Soileau, Joshua Mensch, Ben Williams, Natasha Patel, Hannah Palmer, Jim Gavin, Meg Levad, Molly Antopol, James Arthur, Joshua Rivkin, Sean Hill, Alexandra Teague, Elizabeth Bradfield, Sarah Frisch, Caitlin Cowan, Skip Horack, Shannon Finck, Andrew Zimmerman, Erin Beeghly, Chanda Feldman, John Evans, Jennifer Foerster, and Maria Hummel. Enormous gratitude especially to Jill McDonough and Matt W. Miller for their friendship and support of this book (and New England good times)! And thank you to the women of my Atlanta-based writing group, Narrative Collective, whose friendship has been an unexpected and precious gift of adulthood and who have been reading and helping me shape the poems in this book for years: Stacy Mattingly, Rachael Maddux, Kate Tuttle, Esther Lee, Suzanne Mozes, Melanie Jordan: Warhorse forever.

Many thanks to all in the communities and workshops at UT-Chattanooga, the University of Maryland, the Stegner Program, Bread Loaf, and the Sewanee Writers' Conference. For the gift of full-time employment and health insurance and saving me from the crush of adjunctdom when I needed it most, and for the absolute best colleagues, I'm grateful to the University of West Georgia's English Department. Many thanks to my wonderful colleagues at MIT and the WRAP program—I learned a mind-blowing amount from you and will deeply miss our work together. Thank you to Stanford and the Stegner Program, VCCA, Vermont Studio Center, and Hambidge for the support and space to focus on my writing for extended periods of time and to the Mass Cultural Council and St. Botolph Club Foundation for recent awards that allowed me to keep writing and to keep the faith. Thank you to the Sound Archives at Berea College for a fellowship that led to the birth of Alva. I'm deeply grateful to the Goat Farm in Atlanta for the support of Narrative Collective and for the space to hold our workshops and write for several years. This book wouldn't have happened without that tremendous gift.

As a writer and educator, I recall with so much unending gratitude the teachers whose brilliance and mentoring I carry with me always: Gloria Oster, Richard Jackson, Michael Collier, Joshua Weiner, Elizabeth Arnold, W.S. Di Piero, Earl Braggs, Greg O'Dea. And with deep reverence to the teachers whom I didn't get to thank enough before they left us: Stanley Plumly, Eavan Boland, Robert Duffy, and Gavin Townsend.

And to my oldest friends and co-conspirators from East Tennessee—Jessie Thomas, Niki King-Jones, Jennifer Wonn, and Cicily Newsom—y'all are the smartest, sassiest, most stubborn, most beautiful and hilarious people I know. We've been laughing and crying and trouble-making together for thirty years, and I can't wait for all our adventures in the decades ahead. Thank you for your constant love and friendship. I can't imagine my life without you.

Thank you to my whole family: all the McKees, Daltons, Newberrys, and Miles, and especially my parents, Alice and Richard, for their unconditional love and support and for always modeling kindness and integrity and generosity. You raised us with so much love and that is a gift more precious than any.

I am especially lucky to have such dear friends and fellow writers in my family, too. Beth Newberry: thank you for a lifetime of laughter and amazing conversations about books and love and bourbon and wine. To my sister, Sarah, you are the other half of my brain—my rock, my whole heart. You've been there for all of it, cheering me on, showing up for all the good times and the hard, an absolute badass in everything you do. I'm so lucky to be your sister—the luckiest.

And finally, to my darling Dougie and Alasdair, I started this book in the gaping hole of the-before-you and finished it in the miracle of your presence. I love you.